Original title:
Wristbands and Wishes

Copyright © 2025 Creative Arts Management OÜ
All rights reserved.

Author: Arabella Whitmore
ISBN HARDBACK: 978-1-80586-103-4
ISBN PAPERBACK: 978-1-80586-575-9

Spirals of Spirit

A band so bright, it makes you smile,
Twists and turns, in crazy style.
Holding dreams in a stretchy hug,
With laughs and giggles, it's quite the drug.

Each twist a thought, that bounces back,
If I wear this, I'll find my knack.
With a snap, it shouts out loud,
"Be silly, be bold, be unbowed!"

Manifesting Moments

Here's a charm to catch your glee,
It dances on your wrist, you see.
With every tug, it sparks delight,
As wishes float like kites in flight.

Stretch it wide for hopes to soar,
Wrap it tight for laughs galore.
Bouncing dreams in colors bold,
A bracelet story yet untold!

Colors of Creativity

A rainbow twist upon my arm,
Each hue a laugh, each shade a charm.
Fingers tugging at the bliss,
In spinning circles, dreams can't miss.

With painted hues of joy and cheer,
Each color whispers, "Have no fear!"
Let's dance around in quirky styles,
And strut our stuff for endless miles.

Echoes of Enthusiasm

A jingle here, a jangle there,
With every movement, we declare.
Life's a joke, a playful jest,
Wear your grin, and stand the test.

With bouncy bands of every tone,
They cheer us on, we're never alone.
Laughter ripples with each glance,
Join the party, take a chance!

Symbols of Strength

In the market, bright colors gleam,
People gather, ready to dream.
A rainbow wrapped round my wrist,
Promises made, few can resist.

Laughter echoes, pain takes flight,
With a jolly leap, we take to flight.
Each twist and turn, a silly dance,
In this moment, we take our chance.

Interwoven Intentions

Threads of fate, tangled and sly,
Hopes tied together, reaching the sky.
Jokes abound, with a wink we share,
As giggles escape, pulling hearts bare.

Bouncing ideas, like springy springs,
With each flick, a laughter that sings.
Silly wishes, tangled in thread,
Each knot a giggle, joy widely spread.

Hues of Happiness

Frosty blue or neon green,
Colors dance, so bright, so keen.
With every hue, a grin ensues,
Painting smiles, with every muse.

In the chaos, joy takes hold,
As tales of laughter, brightly unfold.
Each color a chuckle, a reason to cheer,
A splash of humor, always near.

Frameworks of Fulfillment

Crafty designs, we build our dreams,
With every layer, resilience beams.
Laughter structures the paths we take,
In this playground, leaps we make.

With wobbly feet, the giggles rise,
Constructing joy with each surprise.
A framework of fun, we proudly raise,
In a dance of life, we sway and praise.

Weaving the Future

In a land where threads connect,
A tapestry of dreams we respect.
Each knot a hope, each twist a laugh,
Stitching our fates on this crazy path.

From silly bands to colors bright,
We've bound our lives with pure delight.
With every hue, a chuckle blooms,
In this wild world, joy always looms.

Shades of Belief

Pink for giggles, blue for cheer,
Each shade whispers, 'Come, draw near!'
Dare to swap, dare to mix,
Color our lives with playful kicks.

In every shade, a secret quest,
Laughter sparked with every jest.
From marigold to lime so bold,
Our stories shared, our lives unfold.

Hearts Entwined

Looped together in silly style,
Hearts united, oh what a while!
With every twist, a friendship gained,
Through laughter, love, and joy unchained.

In this dance, we laugh out loud,
Joyful shouts, we draw a crowd.
Each tiny band a tale to tell,
In this wild world, we weave so well.

Messages in Multitudes

Each bracelet holds a funny quirk,
Witty phrases that make us smirk.
A message here, a pun out there,
  Sharing laughter everywhere!

We wear our humor, day and night,
With every clasp, we spark delight.
These tiny tokens, oh what a thrill,
Bringing smiles with every drill!

Emblems of Enthusiasm

Strapped on tight for all to see,
A rainbow of joy, quite carefree.
Each charm a tale, a laugh or two,
In this wild ride, we're never through.

Bouncing left and right, what a sight,
They squeak and clink, oh what delight!
When friends unite, the fun's unplanned,
In this crazy world, we take a stand.

Signals of Solace

When life is tough and skies are gray,
These little bands keep gloom at bay.
A giggle here, a nudge right there,
They bring us smiles, they show we care.

In whispered dreams, we share our tales,
With silly jokes that never fails.
For every frown, there's bright reprieve,
These tokens of hope, we all believe.

Tapestry of Tomorrows

In crafty knots, our futures weave,
With colors bold, we dare to dream.
They flutter high on winds of cheer,
Each twinkle tells us, 'Nothing to fear!'

A jester's cap in woven strands,
We prance and dance, our lives in bands.
With every twist, the stories grow,
A tapestry that steals the show.

Colors of Connection

Stripes of pink and shades of blue,
We search for fun in all we do.
Through giggles shared and pranks so sly,
These vibrant links can make us fly.

They stretch and bend, oh what a game,
Reminders of friends who feel the same.
With every tug, a laugh ignites,
In our wacky world, we scale new heights.

Cords of Charisma

In a dance of colors, they twist and twirl,
Each thread a tale, in life's wild whirl.
A jester's grin, a magician's charm,
With each bright band, brings a dose of warm.

Symbols of Serenity

Worn on the arm, like a badge of glee,
A peace treaty forged between you and me.
Bouncing with laughter, they jingle and chime,
As we conjure calm in the chaos of time.

Veils of Vision

Hold tight your dreams with these colorful bands,
They guide our steps with invisible hands.
Magic's in the air, as visions take flight,
With each little charm, we spark our delight.

Bridges of Belonging

From the studio floor to the picnic's spread,
We wear our colors, never filled with dread.
They link us together, a community cheer,
In this vibrant fashion, we dance without fear.

Tokens of Tomorrow

In a world where dreams are made,
We wrap our hopes with a craftsman's aid,
Each color bright, a giggle and glee,
As we leap to future's jamboree.

With charms that jingle, a flippery flair,
Turning frowns into joy; why would we despair?
We toss our plans like confetti in air,
Where laughter blooms and worries beware.

Ribbons of Yearning

In drawer of wishes, a tangle of thread,
Colors of yesteryears, where antics led,
Each loop a chuckle, and each knot a pun,
Winked at the sky 'cause we're all so fun!

We tie our dreams with a jazzy flair,
Snagging giggles in the very air,
In a universe that loves to jest,
Our hopes flutter around, a sunny zest.

Bracelets of Bravery

A wrist adorned with tales untold,
Each bead a giggle, a stumble bold,
We dance in palaces of flair and fun,
Where every mishap shines with the sun.

With glitz and sparkles, we prance and spin,
Daring our fears, not letting them win,
Through laughter we conquer, oh what a sight,
Bracelets of dreams that glow through the night.

Spirit Strings

Strung with laughter, a magical thread,
Tickling hearts, where the silly do tread,
Each twist a giggle, a playful cheer,
See how the joy can wiggle and steer!

We dance on strings of bright delight,
Chasing the shadows, igniting the light,
With every frolic, the world will sway,
Join the parade of quirky bouquet!

Fates Intertwined

In a world where rubber bands cling,
Dreams and laughter dance and swing.
One matched set, a friendship bail,
Tangled thoughts in colors pale.

They stretch and twist, a comical sight,
Holding secrets under the moonlight.
With every tug, a giggle's sound,
In silly bonds, we're tightly wound.

A purple one for chores missed,
A blue for moments full of bliss.
As patterns clash, we shout hooray,
In playful chaos, we find our way.

So let's create this charm parade,
With every loop, our fears invade.
Through every stretch, we'll find our rhyme,
In tangled tales, we'll bide our time.

Colors of Conviction

A rainbow wrapped around my wrist,
Each hue a tale, a quirky twist.
The red for daring, bold and bright,
A yellow laugh in the dreary night.

The green reminds me not to pout,
With every stretch, I scream and shout.
Blue brings calm when life's a race,
While orange sparks a silly face.

Swirling colors, swirling schemes,
A tradition born of silly dreams.
Each laugh shared, a vibrant thread,
In this kaleidoscope, no dread.

So let the shades collide and blend,
Embrace the colors, don't pretend.
With every snap and silly cheer,
We'll keep this laughter, oh so near.

Subtle Signatures

An orange twist, a crimson flash,
We write our stories in a dash.
With every band, each line we pen,
Our silly tales begin again.

A wink, a nod, a playful tease,
In rubber realms, we do as we please.
These little loops, they hold our glee,
As flimsy symbols of our spree.

In secret meetings, they conspire,
Each little bracelet fuels our fire.
With scribbled notes and silly quotes,
We navigate like drifting boats.

So wear these tokens on your sleeve,
With every laugh, you can believe.
In every twist, a secret air,
Together we soar, light as air.

Woven Wishes

A few loose threads, we weave and twine,
With every knot, a dream, divine.
These playful ties, our silly art,
Made of giggles, they set apart.

A little tug, a double knot,
The mishaps shared, forgot on the spot.
With every color, a wish we cast,
As we create memories that last.

In every stretch, a tale unfolds,
Of quirky moments, laughter told.
With every twist, a fortune spun,
Together we laugh, we dancing run.

So let's embrace our tangled fate,
With every snap, we celebrate.
In woven tales, our joy ignites,
From silly bands, we reach new heights.

The Fabric of Fate

In a world where colors blend,
A twist of yarn can make a friend.
With every loop and every thread,
A giggle grows, and worries shed.

Laughter weaves through every seam,
A patchwork quilt of every dream.
It's silly how we tie our luck,
With funny charms and stitches stuck.

Each knot we tie brings tales to tell,
Of tangled yarn and giggles swell.
We dance with joy, a playful spree,
And fate's a jester, wild and free.

So grab a thread and give a twirl,
Embrace the chaos, let it whirl.
For in this fabric, life unwinds,
A tapestry of quirky minds.

Tales of Tomorrow

In the land of listed dreams,
Where every wish comes with a scheme.
We write our hopes on paper strips,
And laugh until we lose our grips.

Tomorrow's tales are often spun,
With silly puns and all-out fun.
We scribble plans with crayons bright,
As bedtime stories take their flight.

Our futures dance in rainbow hues,
With goofy shoes and vibrant views.
Each quirky thought becomes a song,
A melody that's never wrong.

So let the pages turn anew,
In dreams of us and wacky you.
Tomorrow's laughter leads the way,
To wacky fun we'll seize today.

Lives Entangled

Life's a web of playful fates,
With tangled threads and funny traits.
We bump and laugh, and sometimes fall,
Like clumsy clowns at the fun fair's call.

In every twist, a story hides,
Of silly slips and wild rides.
With every giggle, bonds are made,
In this snare where Jesters played.

Our paths entwined like silly string,
In every mishap, joy will cling.
We dance through chaos, side by side,
No finer ride, we'll take in stride.

So here's to life, both odd and grand,
To every little silly plan.
Together we may trip and sway,
But laughter leads us on the way.

Lines of Light

In beams of joy, we find our way,
With giggles brightening the gray.
A doodled dream, a sparkly line,
We draw our fate, a grand design.

Lines of laughter crisscross time,
A silly dance, a twist in rhyme.
With every chuckle echoes glow,
As friendships bloom and spirits grow.

We sketch our thoughts on life's great page,
In colors bold, we take the stage.
With hidden pranks and playful glee,
Our lines unite in harmony.

So let the light dance from the heart,
In this bright scrimmage, none apart.
For in these lines, our joys ignite,
In every smile, we share the light.

Charms of Desire

In a land where charms all dawdle,
Wore a ring that caused a wrangle.
"Whose luck is this?" they cried with glee,
As it pulled folks like ants to a spree.

The squirrel upturned the table's dish,
"A pocket's home for every wish!"
With a laugh, the chickens took to flight,
In search of dreams that shine so bright.

A cat in boots gave a wink and said,
"Wishes are fun when light as bread!"
They plotted a scheme for the next parade,
With cookies and charms, and lemonade.

But as the day turned into night,
Not one charm glimmered in the light.
"Let's swap our pieces, let's have some fun,
Tomorrow, my friends, the race is on!"

Bands of Belief

A jester danced with bands so bold,
Each twist and twine, a story told.
"I've got a hunch this one will cheer,"
He tugged too hard, flew through the rear.

The elephant joined, with great delight,
Wearing colors far too bright.
"Can these hold me?" he questioned the sky,
As onlookers laughed, "Just give it a try!"

The sloth kicked back, with a band in tow,
"We'll see who's fastest, give it a go!"
The race began with a pouch of cheese,
And chaos erupted like a summer breeze.

So here's to trust in bands we wear,
For laughter is wealth when you're light as air.
Join in the fun, let the party start,
With ribbons of humor, woven to heart.

Emblems of Aspirations

A penguin dreamed of skies so blue,
Stitched an emblem, oh so askew!
"I'll fly tomorrow," he shouted loud,
As the fish all gathered, quite a crowd.

A giraffe peered down from the trees,
"May I borrow that? Pretty please!"
With a wink, the penguin tossed it high,
"Oh no! It landed in... a pie!"

The baker laughed with flour on nose,
"An emblem of dreams, I suppose!"
With each slice served, they found their fate,
In a pastry realm, who wouldn't wait?

So chase your dreams, no matter how odd,
In silly places, give a nod.
Emblems will guide with giggles and cheer,
Disarray your hopes, still feel near!

Ties of Fate

A silly cat wore ties like bows,
Upon his collar, everyone knows.
With each new twist, a new surprise,
As laughter sparkled in everyone's eyes.

The dog next door, with a wagging tail,
Joined the parade, donned a big mail.
"I'll send a wish to the moon tonight,
With starlit ties, let's take flight!"

They spun in circles, making a mess,
Chasing each other, oh, what finesse!
"Hold on tight!" the cat let out a yelp,
As they tumbled down, a giggly help.

With ties of laughter, they danced till dawn,
In wacky patterns, to the breaking lawn.
So tie your dreams with joy and glee,
And let the fates tie your hearts, you'll see!

Threads of Tomorrow

In colors bright, we tie our fate,
A twist, a knot, at the old school gate.
With each new loop, a laugh we share,
No fashion show, just who really cares?

What secrets hide in strands so tight?
They dance and jiggle, pure delight.
Our future woven with hopes and cheese,
Oh, look! A pigeon, right under the trees!

We'll wear them proud, though they may clash,
Like socks on hands, or a mash-up of trash.
But each vibrancy tells its own jest,
Together we shine, it's simply the best!

So here's to all, with knots that gleam,
Let's settle down for a silly dream.
With threads that stretch through thick and thin,
We'll laugh our way to next weekend's win!

Bands of Unity

Gather round, with laughs to spare,
A colorful mix, like mismatched hair.
One size fits all? That's quite a joke,
Especially when they choke the bloke!

Like rubber ducks in a wobbly race,
We squawk and bounce, it's a silly place.
Linked together, side by side,
With goofy grins, and arms open wide.

A stretchy band, so meant to break,
Yet here we are, for friendship's sake.
Each pull and stretch, a story told,
With giggles echoing, hearts of gold.

So let's rejoice in this wacky crew,
With endless antics and more than a few.
Unified we stand, in all we do,
In a world of chaos, we'll make do!

Dreams Threaded

Imagine dreams like swirly fries,
Curly and crispy, oh what a prize!
Each twirl a wish, a laugh ignites,
In the midnight glow, under twinkling lights.

We strut the streets with whims so grand,
A carnival vibe, you'll want to stand.
With quirky fantasies tied to our hands,
In this realm of fun, we make our plans.

Like art on a fridge, it's all a mess,
Yet every piece is pure happiness.
Every twist tells a tale in hue,
Of hopes that bounce like a kangaroo!

So take a bow with your colorful flair,
Let's paint the sky, no need to care.
For in this dream, we reign supreme,
Laughter and joy are the ultimate theme!

Notes of Nuance

A jingle here, a jangle there,
Notes that dance like they just don't care.
Each twist and turn, a playful sound,
A symphony of joy, swirling all around.

With mismatched socks and hats askew,
We prance and hop, it's quite the view.
Tune in for giggles, a silly spree,
As laughter bubbles, can't 'contain' me!

Who knew a tune could bring such glee?
With tunes so vibrant, we all agree.
Strummed from the heart, just like a cat,
The funniest thing since that time with the hat!

So raise your voice, let spirits soar,
In this quirky tune, we'll laugh some more.
With notes of nuance, we'll strut and play,
Making memories in our own funny way!

Nexus of Notions

A flick of color on your arm,
Each hue a promise, bright and warm.
A band for luck, another for style,
Worn with a wink, and a goofy smile.

They say the green brings wealth, oh dear!
But transitive luck just disappeared.
With each new clasp, we change our fate,
But only for snacks on a dinner plate.

Adventures waiting, wrist-locked tight,
Every single band feels just so right.
Mismatched colors, a neon sight,
A fashion statement in day or night.

At times, they break; just witness the fate,
Pieces of memories lie in wait.
Collecting dust, but that's okay,
Tomorrow's laughter saves the day.

Tapestry of Ties

A rainbow universe, wrapped on your skin,
With each tiny clasp, we let the fun begin.
Some symbolize joy, some act as a curse,
Who knew such flair could equal such verse?

Lost the pink charm? It's not far astray,
On the couch, stuck with crumbs from today.
An arm full of stories, not one's a bore,
Now mixing and matching is never a chore.

Exchange them like secrets, some giggles and laughs,
Ties woven with dreams, and some silly gaffes.
Every layer whispers some mischief and cheer,
A colorful journey, let's crank up the gear!

With every twist and a silly dance,
Who knew good fortune wore a comfy pants?
Unraveled, yet tangled, a joyful surprise,
With ties that connect us, we're wise to the skies.

Energies of Empathy

Bright little bands, they jump and they sway,
Like pep in our step on a shiny new day.
One says 'hello,' the next 'be my mate,'
Together they giggle; isn't that great?

Each wrist bears tales of mischief, delight,
A band for the silly, and one for the fright.
Though sometimes it's awkward, or one gets too tight,
We stretch out for hugs, taking flight in the night.

A party of hints wrapped snug on our sleeves,
With quirky designs, and a few loopy leaves.
Why wear just one when you can sport them all?
Like marbles in pockets, we'll stand proud and tall!

With colors of friendship, they dance and they spin,
Each childlike wonder, where do we begin?
A chuckle, a charm, and a lot of joy,
We'll share all our laughter, just girl and a boy.

Lives in Layers

A rainbow of fortune, wrapped on a twist,
Each loop holds a giggle, none can be missed.
A fuchsia for flair, a blue for the chill,
Every layer whispers, 'Let's climb up that hill!'

A friend likes to know just what I lack,
She ties up her hopes, she's got my back.
Colors spin tales under the sun,
When bands come together, we frolic and run.

Scrambled in laughter, we trade and we share,
A layer of fun, hanging loose in the air.
Like origami dreams folded up with glee,
Each sketch of our lives writes the fun's decree.

And when the sunset calls us to rest,
Our bands still vibrate, feeling so blessed.
With each clink and a clatter, we echo our cheer,
Wearing love and laughter like a badge of the year.

Holders of Hopes

On a wrist, a colorful band,
Holding dreams that are all planned.
Every color tells a tale,
Like a fish that tripped and fell.

With a tug, the wishes fly,
Like a kite that soars up high.
It giggles as it waves goodbye,
Oh the wisdom in this tie!

Once it's on, you're bound to smile,
Finding joys in every mile.
If you trip, just strike a pose,
Dance it off, that's how it goes!

In the end, it's just a string,
Yet it holds the joy we bring.
With each snap, a laugh we weave,
Coz sometimes life's a trick or cleave.

Patterns of Promise

A dotted line upon my wrist,
Holds the giggles, can't resist.
Patterned stripes, oh what a sight,
Makes even Mondays feel so bright.

Each twist and turn a silly dream,
Like a fish that loves to gleam.
What's that? A tiny duck parade,
In my mind, a fun charade!

I wear them like they're badges, see?
Silly thoughts, oh let them be!
Every pull, a poke at fate,
With a wink of joy innate.

Layers thick with laughter's thread,
What was once a thought now sped.
The pattern's more than what it seems,
It's a quilt of all my dreams!

Strings of Serenity

A twinkling string, so light and fun,
Swinging like a playful pun.
Wrapped around with giggles tight,
In the day or in the night.

Each color shouts a little cheer,
Like a clown that draws us near.
A tickle, twist, and funny faces,
As silly thoughts fill all the spaces.

When it snaps, I just must grin,
Like a cat that's caught its chin.
Every little tale I share,
Brings a puddle of laughter here!

While they dangle, carefree roam,
Every step, a goofy poem.
In this string I find my grace,
And a silly, happy place!

Signals of Sentiment

A colorful signal on my wrist,
Winks and flirts, you can't resist.
It hums a tune when I shake,
Like a dancing slice of cake!

Living in this quirkiness,
Every day's a state of bliss.
When I trip, it sings out loud,
"Oh my goodness, look at you, proud!"

Wearing joy like it's a trend,
Like a wink from a long-lost friend.
Every pull a little giggle,
Imbued with charm that makes me wiggle.

Oh the tales these colors weave,
Of silly pranks that we believe.
With each twist, the laughter flows,
In this bright place, joy only grows.

Passages of Possibility

In a land where dreams run wild,
Each color tells a tale,
A swirl of hopes wrapped tight,
In stretchy bands that never fail.

You slip one on, feel the glow,
A hundred wishes in a twist,
Try not to lose it, oh no,
That'd be a real plot twist!

If only life was like a game,
Where every charm brings cheer,
But instead, we chase the same,
And trip on all we hold dear.

So laugh and stretch with all your might,
Each loop is filled with glee,
As dreams take flight in party light,
Unraveled, oh so carefree!

Bracelets of Belief

They sparkle like a thousand stars,
Each twist a secret plan,
With every flick, you're closer, far,
To be the very best, you can!

Wrapped around your wrist so snug,
A laugh escapes, a giggle light,
You dance and twirl, unleash the bug,
With every wish, your heart takes flight.

Just don't let it slip away,
Or you might lose your way,
They're more than just a bright display,
They're like your inner sunray!

So stack them high, wear them bold,
Each strand a story to unfold,
In colors loud, a sight to behold,
A festival of fun, pure gold!

Symbols of Stardust

Tiny trinkets shine and sway,
With every wish, they seem to wink,
In a cosmic dance, they play,
A giggle and a joyful clink.

They hold the tales of laughter bright,
In splendid hues and funky tones,
As dreams take flight beneath the night,
Leaving behind the mundane tones.

What if one granted you a laugh?
A tickle, twist, or silly dance?
You'd pop and spin like a giraffe,
In a world of sheer mischance!

So twirl and jump, don't hold it back,
These charms bring joy and fun,
Embrace the quirk, stay on track,
As life's a jest, a joyous run!

Chains of Change

Linked together in a silly way,
Each jangle tells a funny tale,
What's in a clasp? Just shades of play,
As whimsy winds like a playful gale.

One glance can spark a hearty cheer,
A hook, a latch, a playful dance,
With every charm, you stoke the sphere,
Of pure, unfiltered happenstance.

Some are bright, and some just shine,
Each one a playful little tease,
In this game, they all align,
As laughter floats on a warm breeze.

So let them jingle, let them sway,
And dance to beats only they know,
In chains of fun, we laugh and play,
As life becomes a grand cabaret!

Links of Light

A twist of colors on my arm,
Each hue a giggle, a tiny charm.
Friends gather 'round in a swirling mess,
Laughing at wishes, we surely bless.

Silly secrets hidden in knots,
Like tying shoelaces, we forget our thoughts.
Hopes wrapped in laughter like a gift,
Each strand a moment, ready to lift.

Wishing on colors that fade and glow,
In a dance of joy, we twirl and flow.
Holding tight to dreams like bouncing ball,
With every tug, we stand up tall.

Our stories tangled, but that's just fine,
Life's a party; come sip the wine!
With fraying edges and ties that break,
We laugh at the mess, for friendship's sake.

Anchors of Ambition

Tied on my wrist, a captain's flair,
With every leap, we sail the air.
Hopes like boats on a wavy sea,
Anchored in laughter, just you and me.

With comical capers and silliness grand,
We set our course, hand in hand.
Chasing the wind on a playful breeze,
In this life's race, we'll never tease.

Oh, the tales in knots and bends,
Like pirate maps with funky ends.
Sailing through mishaps, gleefully bold,
Our fortunes gleaming, not bought or sold.

Tethered by humor, we rise so high,
In a world that spins, we'll catch the sky.
So come aboard, let joy unfurl,
With anchors firm, we'll rule this world!

Patterns of Possibility

Weaving dreams in colors bright,
Laughter twirls in every sight.
Doodles dance on my wrist so snug,
A comic twist, a friendly hug.

Fancy patterns that don't quite match,
But hey, darling, here's the catch!
In each weirdness, we find our groove,
Silly magic in every move.

Oh, to tie wishes in loops and swirls,
Like confetti tossed by giggling girls.
Each twist a chuckle, a sunny jest,
A riot of fun, never a test.

With possibilities bursting like soap,
In every color, we twist and hope.
Not one straight line, but zigzag cheer,
In our funny world, it's the joy we steer!

Dreamcatchers of the Soul

Tangled catchers hung so bright,
Sifting through dreams in the moonlight.
With each silly snag, a chuckle flows,
Like catching laughter in a colorful prose.

Wishes tangled like a cat's soft paw,
Playing with yarn, a giggling awe.
With every loop, our tales unspool,
In a dreamy whirl, we play the fool.

Finding joy in the sweetest slips,
Chasing laughter with playful quips.
These radiant knots, they sparkle and gleam,
In our buffet of hope, we delight and beam.

So here's to dreamers, odd and cool,
With a dash of whimsy, let's bend the rule.
In this giggly realm, our spirits whole,
We catch the stars with our jolly soul!

Bands of Kindness

In a world of hues so bright,
A secret pact we might ignite.
On our wrists the colors cling,
Promises of joy they bring.

With every twist and every turn,
These joyful loops help us learn.
To laugh at life's absurdity,
And dance in silly solidarity.

A pink one says 'let's make a joke',
While green proclaims 'let's share a poke'.
These ties of cheer, they hold us tight,
Radiating laughter, day and night.

So wear them high and wear them proud,
Let commonplace be unallowed.
A band of colors, a splash of fun,
Together we'll shine like the sun.

Links of Longing

When boredom strikes, oh what a mess,
A longing grows, we must confess.
These little loops pull tight and twist,
Creating plans we can't resist.

A blue one sings of ice cream dreams,
While tangled thoughts burst at the seams.
Our quirky quests commence right here,
Each thread a story full of cheer.

From merry moments, bonds we weave,
A silly prank, we can achieve.
Combined we stretch across the night,
In colors bold, we take flight.

Let's craft a saga, bright and wide,
With every laugh, we throw aside.
Those links of play hold magic true,
Together we'll find what's bold and new.

Cords of Courage

These vibrant threads are more than style,
They give us strength, they make us smile.
A hint of courage pulled so tight,
In awkward moments, we ignite.

When fears arise, don't you fret,
Just tug the cord, remember yet.
Each knot a tale of bravery,
Each loop a guide through savagery.

Adventures call, we may just trip,
But snugly held, we'll never slip.
Colors bind like cheers of friends,
With laughter shared, the fun extends.

Jump and jive with all our might,
Together we'll shine, oh what a sight!
In every twist, in every bend,
These cords of courage never end.

Embrace of Endeavors

In every task, there's a goofy spark,
A chance to play, to leave our mark.
This woven charm whispers out loud,
Encouragement for every crowd.

With colors fair, we take a stand,
United we craft, hand in hand.
Mishaps become the best of tales,
With laughter loud, we lift the scales.

From clumsy falls to silly fun,
We'll cheer each other, everyone.
An embrace of dreams, all out there,
In joyful chaos, we share a flare.

So roll your sleeves and bring your quirk,
In every endeavor, let's not shirk.
Together we'll chase the silliest things,
With warm embrace, oh how life sings.

Hues of the Heart

In colors bright, we wear our joys,
With laughter loud, we laugh like boys.
A rainbow wraps around our wrist,
Each shade a tale, a funny twist.

Blue for goof-ups, red for glee,
Green for snacks, oh come with me!
We dance and twirl, a sight to see,
With every shade, our spirits free.

A splash of yellow, a pinch of gray,
We twinkle and shine throughout the day.
With crafty charms and silly dreams,
Life's just better than it seems!

So wear those hues, take not a pause,
For every giggle, there's a cause.
With heart's own palette, bright and bold,
Our painted laughs will never fold.

Gifts of the Present

Tied up in bows, these gifts galore,
With tape and ribbons you might explore.
A box for socks, with a funny note,
And there's a cat that loves to gloat.

I thought of you when spanning far,
Sent cupcake socks, how bizarre!
With every laugh, another cheer,
Unwrap the silly, shed a tear.

These objects blend absurd and sweet,
A rubber chicken? Ain't that neat?
Forget the past, let's laugh today,
For joy's the fruit, come what may!

So gather round, unwrap the fun,
A treasure hunt for everyone!
With silly gifts, we'll keep the jest,
In the present's arms, we're truly blessed.

Unseen Bindings

Invisible threads, they twist and twine,
They hold us close, like a funny line.
A wink, a nod, a silly grin,
The bonds we share, oh let's begin.

A nudge here, a poke there,
With gregarious glee, we throw in flair.
With just a glance, we know the cue,
To fall apart—what a hullabaloo!

We dance through life, like jesters roam,
These bindings, they take us far from home.
With laughter loud, we break the chains,
In funny antics, joy remains.

So let's celebrate all ties unseen,
In this wacky world, we're evergreen.
With every folly, we take our stance,
Each giggle stitches a new dance.

Journeys Imprinted

On paths unknown, we stomp and leap,
With memories made, that we can keep.
Each step a giggle, and a new trip,
Our funny tales, they surely rip!

From sandcastles to pizza lines,
With maps unwritten, we find new signs.
Our journey's dance is wildly clear,
Each twist and turn, brings out the cheer.

We laugh with ducks, and slip on pies,
The road ahead is filled with sighs.
Yet every stumble turns to gold,
As funny stories are retold.

So take a step, let laughter flow,
With every footprint, watch it grow.
Our journeys mark the smiles we wear,
Together we weave our funny flair.

Tokens of Transformation

In the land of colorful ties,
Bright dreams dance in our eyes.
With a flick and a twist,
We summon the magic we can't resist.

Laughter echoes in the air,
As we twirl without a care.
A spectrum of joy on our skin,
Whispering secrets of where we've been.

From purple to blue, and green to red,
Each hue tells tales of the things we've said.
They shrink when we sweat, stretch when we play,
A rubbery charm that won't fade away.

With each snap, a new story starts,
Turning our frowns into colorful arts.
So, let's wear our tales like a crown,
Hoping laughter will never let us down.

Luminescent Links

A flicker of glow in the dark of night,
These little gems are quite the sight.
They shimmer and shine with a giggly glee,
While swaying gently like grass by the tree.

With every tug, there comes a grin,
As silly mischief invites us in.
A dance of colors, a burst of fun,
Who knew bonding could be this pun?

Stretching way beyond our expectations,
Creating moments and silly sensations.
They stretch our laughter and glow in haste,
Turning ordinary times into a joyous feast.

So here's to the links that keep us lit,
In a world of giggles, don't ever quit!
Plus, they double as handy doodads galore,
Stretched out or snapped, we couldn't ask for more!

Fairytales in Fabric

Stitched together with tales of delight,
These bands hold stories that take flight.
With whispers of magic in every fold,
They spin funny yarns just waiting to be told.

Unicorns prancing? Why, yes, they do!
Adventures await; oh, where to pursue?
With a tug and a twist, you'll laugh a bit loud,
As these fabric friends make even trolls proud.

From dragon rides to princess quests,
We're bound by the fabric that never rests.
Each twist a giggle, each stretch a cheer,
Making memories in this laughter sphere.

So let's scribble dreams and stitch them tight,
In this fairytale world, everything feels right.
A fabric of friendships with giggles to share,
We're spinning joy everywhere we dare!

Hopes in Harmony

In the jangle of colors, there's magic afloat,
Each band a dream, each wish our note.
Tickling our hopes, like laughter on a breeze,
These playful charms bring us to our knees.

Plenty of giggles as we bounce along,
With every hue, we dance to the song.
From silly to serious, all in a row,
They tie our wishes with a whimsical glow.

In the merry chaos, we tie our fate,
With pranks and laughter—we create!
Each color a hope, each band a plan,
Crafting a future that's clever and grand.

So let's wear our wishes with smiles so bright,
Turning every moment into pure delight.
In this colorful rhythm, we won't be shy,
For laughter and love will always fly high!

Gems of Gratitude

On my wrist, they clatter and jingle,
Each one holds a promise to mingle.
I wear them for luck, or so they say,
But mostly for style on a casual day.

When I clap my hands, they all make a sound,
Like a chorus of laughter that's joyfully found.
I'll trade you a charm for a slice of pie,
But you better be quick, or I'll say goodbye!

Each gem has a tale, a quirk of its own,
A bit like my friends, but much more prone.
To slip and slide on my wrist they do dance,
Chasing away my I-can't-find-my-pants stance.

So here's to the bangles, the beads, and the bling,
Each one a giggle, a joyous little fling.
I collect them all, like coins in a jar,
Together they shine, and yes, they are bizarre.

Cords of Connection

In shades of delight, they wrap 'round my skin,
A tangled up web, where silliness begins.
Sometimes they tangle, sometimes they fight,
Like my cat with a ball of yarn at night.

Friendship's the knot, that we tie so tight,
Pulling us closer, making wrongs feel right.
I gave one to Tim, but he lost it in grass,
Now he wears a frown, while I'm having a blast!

Every twist, every loop, a laugh or a grin,
A reminder that life's a grand game to win.
If you hear a thud, it's my cords on the floor,
Dancing to music, but tripping for sure!

So let's twirl and frolic with all of our flair,
In this bright little game, we have life to share.
I'll tie on a cord, and then give you a wink,
Together we'll giggle, till we can't even think!

Tokens of Belief

Little charms that dangle and dance,
Each one a magic, a whimsical chance.
I found one that's blue, and it says "be brave,"
I wore it while jumping—oh, what a wave!

Gift from a friend, it sparkles with cheer,
But watch it closely; it might disappear.
Caught in a dream, or lost in a game,
The tokens remind me that life's not the same.

We swap them like secrets, in laughter we trust,
Each little trinket, a bond that's a must.
I've got one for courage, another for fun,
But mostly it's giggles; oh, we've just begun!

So here's to the curious, the silly, the sweet,
Each token a moment, a memory neat.
Let's trade 'em around till our hearts are aglow,
In the carnival of life, we just steal the show!

Strands of Serenity

A strand around my wrist, so full of glee,
It whispers in colors, 'Just be free!'
When life gets too serious, I give it a tug,
And feel like a child wrapped up in a hug.

Each thread tells a story, of laughter and cheer,
They twirl like the thoughts that bring me near.
I wore one while dancing, fell right on my face,
But up I got laughing, it's all part of grace.

With every new loop, a fresh giggle's born,
I'll craft a new strand from the glow of the dawn.
They may look like chaos, a bit like my life,
But that's where the magic cuts through all the strife!

So here's to the colors, the laughter they bring,
Each twist is a moment, and oh how they sing!
In the realm of the silly, we'll wander and play,
With strands of delight, let's chase gloom away!

Chains of Innocence

On my arm, a stretch of colors bright,
A rainbow in a world that's often white.
Each adds a layer to my story's frame,
And makes my fashion sense wholly a game.

When friends all gather for a giggle-fest,
We swap and trade as we all jest.
It's not just style; it's our secret pact,
A bond so silly, a matter of fact.

Some say they're silly, just plastic and thread,
But they hold the laughter and secrets we've said.
In a world so serious, I wear them with glee,
These chains of innocence, oh so carefree!

So let the world frown, let the critics scoff,
I'm living the dream, and I'll never take off.
Each little trinket, a jolly old jest,
With each tug and pull, life's simply the best!

Mementos of Meaning

A splash of chaos on my wrist so bold,
Each color tells stories, waiting to unfold.
Gifts from my pals, with a wink and a grin,
Collecting these artifacts, oh where to begin?

There's one from the beach, with sand still inside,
And another from last year's wild carnival ride.
Each twist and turn makes a memory tease,
Reminding me always to laugh and to squeeze.

What's that on my arm? A pet rock now lost,
And a charm shaped like cheese, oh, what a cost!
They jangle and dangle, a symphony sweet,
Each memento a giggle, oh, what a treat!

So when all are gathered, let stories ignite,
We share silly tales that stretch through the night.
In this gang of misfits, I thoroughly trust,
With each little token, our laughter is a must!

Captured Hopes

With each little loop, a hope I do stash,
Tied up by colors that really clash.
Expect the weird, oh don't you forget,
My arm's the zoo of dreams, a colorful pet!

One's got a dragon, another a shroom,
Each holds a secret — a wish in full bloom.
Let's tap the fortune, maybe dance on a star,
In the circus of life, you're the best by far!

Silly sequins sparkle, light up my way,
I'll ride this wild whimsy, come what may.
When I flaunt this art, in the sunlight so bright,
I'm the queen of the circus, oh what a sight!

So gather your dreams in these tangled strands,
We'll laugh at the madness, join in with our hands.
With each little flash, a moment to cheer,
In the circus of life, let's make it unclear!

Emblems of Emotion

Look at my wrist, a riot of cheer,
A hodgepodge of heart, all gathered here.
Each little emblem, a giggle in tow,
With bling and some bumps, oh, what a show!

There's one for my cat who thinks he can fly,
And one for that time I nearly said bye.
They chuckle and chatter, these bits of my life,
Turning frowns into laughter, no hint of strife.

Each tangled string holds a secret delight,
A tale of confusion, played out in flight.
So when someone asks, "What's that glow on your arm?"

I just flash a grin, it's my charm and my warm!

So let's toast to chaos, embrace all the fun,
With each silly bauble, our jest has begun.
In these moments of joy, I'll gladly invest,
With each twist and twirl, I'm truly blessed!

Emblems of Enchantment

In colors bright, they wrap around,
Making promises without a sound.
Each little charm, a secret told,
Tickling dreams, like stories of old.

A bangle here, a trinket there,
Dancing on wrists without a care.
They jingle loud, a playful tune,
Spreading laughter from dusk till noon.

Each one a wish, though slightly bent,
In the oddest shapes, what chaos they invent!
A rainbow of hopes on a single thread,
Each twist and turn, a giggle ahead.

So wear your joy, let it parade,
In this circus of fun we've made.
With every shake, let troubles flee,
For magic lives in silly glee.

Embraces of Destiny

Tangled threads in a comical mess,
Yet hold the dreams we long to confess.
From rubber bands to silly beads,
Crafting moments like playful seeds.

Remember the time they turned our hair?
A crown of rubber, quite the affair!
Wrapped 'round our wrists, doing the jig,
Our laughter echoed; we danced a big gig.

Meetings with fate, oh what a laugh,
With goofy charms and a crazy craft.
Every color a quirk, a playful hour,
Sprinkling delight like magical flour.

So let us bind these silly dreams,
In a world where nothing's as it seems.
With every wink and every grin,
We'll wear these tokens; let joy begin!

Woven Whispers

Threads of laughter and mischief spin,
Tied around limbs, where fun begins.
Each little whisper, a funny tale,
Of goofy friends and wild detail.

Like spaghetti knots in a culinary show,
Our dreams twist together, with style and flow.
Holding tales of where we've been,
In this playful journey, we always win.

Celebrate quirks, let the giggles rise,
For these tokens of folly are quite the prize.
A tapestry of joy, bright and bold,
In every color, our antics unfold.

So shake off the gloom, let laughter roam,
These woven stories bring us home.
With every flick, a chuckle returns,
In the fabric of life, our spirit burns.

Mementos of Magic

In a land where silly reigns supreme,
Tiny treasures fuel the dream.
Bobbing and weaving, they come alive,
Our goofy trinkets help us thrive.

Catch a laugh on a swirling clasp,
Or wear a grin tight, give it a grasp.
Odd little tokens, they're quite the find,
Making us chuckle, feeling aligned.

A dance here, a twirl there too,
Each merry memento whispers who knew?
With every flick, let the laughter lead,
For in this carnival, we plant a seed.

So let's toast our quirks, raise a cheer,
For every charm, let's hold it dear.
Embrace the silliness, let's all play,
In this magical moment, let's seize the day!

Crystals of Connection

In a colorful daze, we dance and twirl,
Elastic charms brighten each boy and girl.
Laughing together, we make quite a scene,
Tangled in laughter, oh what a routine!

A friend wore a bracelet, a dazzling delight,
But tripped on a shoelace and took quite a flight.
With charms in the air, we all had to cheer,
He landed in cupcakes, oh dear, oh dear!

We shared our good vibes, stacked high on our hands,
As memes came to life from our distant lands.
Each pop of a bubble, we clapped and we cheered,
They sparkled and giggled, just as we feared!

But when one got lost, it led to a quest,
Finding that charm made us laugh at our best.
The search turned to chaos, a comical chase,
For in the end, it was stuffed in a vase!

Whispers of Wisdom

A tiny sage told us, 'Wear this with flair,'
And so we adorned, feeling light as the air.
With whispers of wisdom, we danced in the sun,
Joking that all of our wisdom was done!

Collecting our trinkets, we crafted a code,
Each bead held a secret, or maybe a road.
But once we found out the truths from our fate,
They laughed at our choices, oh this could be fate!

We tossed all our doubts, like seeds in the breeze,
Creating a tale that would aim to please.
But when one went missing, the drama unfurled,
Turns out it was snagged on a passing girl's swirl!

From laughter to fortune, our dreams flew high,
Stitched from the stories that never ran dry.
In this circus of charms, we surely did find,
That humor in moments can lighten the mind!

Journeys Interwoven

With colors so bright, we set out to roam,
Through streets filled with laughter, we felt right at home.
Each step held a story, a goofy headline,
Interwoven adventures, oh how they shine!

We mingled with critters, like squirrels with a plan,
Trading our secrets, like cookies, they ran.
But one fell asleep, in a pile of sweet foam,
And woke up with gum in a young neighbor's comb!

We chalked up confessions on sidewalks so wide,
With jokes that reflected this whimsical ride.
Caught in a moment, we snapped a few pics,
As dots turned to dashes, we danced with our tricks!

From echoes of laughter to tales in the night,
We cherished each moment, our spirits so bright.
For journeys, both silly and wise, we agree,
Are woven together like threads in a spree!

Hopes Intertwined

Worn on my wrist, a colorful band,
It's a promise, a dream, somewhat unplanned.
Every color tells tales of joy and of cheer,
Faded reminders of hopes that are near.

With each silly charm, I dance through the day,
In a circus of wishes, come join in the play.
Juggling these dreams like a clown on the run,
Who knew that such trinkets could be so much fun?

My friends roll their eyes at my colorful flair,
"What's next?" they ask, "Are you weaving your hair?"
But each twist and knot holds a story so bright,
Like a tapestry woven with laughter and light.

So I flaunt my adornments, a quirky delight,
With a wink and a giggle, I take off in flight.
In this world of whimsy, my dreams intertwine,
Wrist-bound adventures, oh, how they shine!

Threads of Time

In the fashion of fortune, I tie on a thread,
Wrapped around hopes, where my thoughts can be fed.
Colors of whimsy, patterns that gleam,
A patchwork of moments that burst into dream.

Tick-tock goes the universe's grand clock,
Each stitch a reminder, a little tick-tock.
Funny how time's just a loop in disguise,
Worn on my arm where my mischief resides.

With each flick of my wrist, the memories fly,
Reminders of laughter that make spirits high.
Caught in a spiral of giggles and fun,
Every little bobble, a laugh to be spun.

So here's to the charms, the jokes that ensue,
My arm's like a canvas, painted bright and true.
Let's dance through our dreams, weaving tales with a grin,

In this silly creation, let the fun begin!

Threads of Hope

A tangle of ribbons, each one a bright dream,
Twisted together in a whimsical scheme.
Worn like a beacon, they shimmer and glow,
Each strand holds a giggle, ready to flow.

When life gives me lemons, I tie a new knot,
Bright colors remind me of laughter I've caught.
In the circus of life, each wish plays a part,
Dancing with humor, a carnival heart!

My friends find it funny, this wrist of delight,
They join in the fun, oh what a sight!
We're tangled in laughter, like vines that entwine,
Spinning our wishes, in this merry design.

So here's to the bands, let them twirl and spin,
Life's colorful journey is where we begin.
With threads of bright hope, we rustle and cheer,
In a world full of magic, let's spread the cheer!

Echoes of Dreams

With bands of bright folly, we dance through the night,
Tangled in laughter, everything feels right.
Echoes of wishes afloat in the breeze,
Each one a chuckle that puts hearts at ease.

Adventurous spirits, we twirl and we leap,
Wrist-bound giggles, we joyfully keep.
In this playful ballet, we share our delight,
Every twinkling moment is a pure delight.

Worn like a badge, here's my rainbow array,
A badge of our friendship, come dance and play.
For every bright color that catches the light,
A memory dances, our future feels bright.

So let the echoes of laughter ring clear,
With each silly knot, let's spread the cheer.
In this carnival of joys where dreams take their flight,
We'll treasure each moment, dancing into the night!

Threads of Hope

In a world of colors bright,
A tangled mess brings great delight.
A twist, a turn, what will it be?
A jester's joke for you and me.

With threads that stretch and sometimes snap,
We wear our laughter like a cap.
Each stitch a thought, a silly rhyme,
Embrace the wobbles, it's just fine!

When fate's a game of hide and seek,
We strap on joy, not fear or bleak.
A little knot, a little cheer,
We dance through life, no need to fear!

So grab your coil, let giggles flow,
In every loop, let laughter grow.
With threads that bind us hand in hand,
We'll weave our dreams in silly strands.

Charms of Desire

A bauble here, a trinket there,
Bouncing thoughts dance in the air.
Quirky ideas line up to play,
In a parade of charm today!

With each little charm, a story spins,
Of mischief, giggles, and goofy wins.
They jingle and jangle like cheerful bells,
Telling secrets, oh, what tales!

A wish for cake? A wish for socks?
We charm our life in silly blocks.
With every clasp, a chuckle, a grin,
Sparkling moments, where do we begin?

So twirl your charms in the sun's warm light,
Each glint a memory, oh what a sight!
Let laughter guide us, let joy compose,
In the garden of dreams, hilariously grow!

Bands of Dreams

A colorful band around my wrist,
A quirky thought that can't be missed.
It bounces up and down with glee,
"Let's be silly!" it shouts to me!

We dance in circles, round and round,
Our silly dreams just know no bound.
With every jolt, a giggle escapes,
Life's a carnival, with funny shapes!

Beneath the stars, we set our sights,
On magic moments, giggling nights.
A twist, a pull, hold on tight,
Our dreams leap forth, a joyous flight!

With bands that move and bend with ease,
We'll paint our world with playful tease.
In every jingle, joy we find,
In the bands of dreams, our hearts aligned.

Ties of Tomorrow

We tie our hopes with ribbons bright,
A goofy mix, oh what a sight!
In a dance that sways like jellybeans,
We laugh and giggle in our routines.

With every knot, a story told,
Of futures bold and joys of old.
We leap and tug at life's great seam,
In a fabric woven with silly dreams!

So grab your tie, don't let it slip,
We're sailing forth on a wobbly ship.
Each twist a chance, a merry chance,
In the ties of tomorrow, let's take a dance!

With laughter ringing clear and loud,
Our bonds of joy will make us proud.
So hold on tight, don't let them go,
In this whimsical ride, we steal the show!

Echoes of Endeavors

In a world of colors bright,
I wore a pledge, such a sight.
Each flick and twist, a ticklish dance,
My dreams were strapped in a silly trance.

A fuchsia flair that squeaked and popped,
On my wrist, it flopped and dropped.
Every wish, a giggle invested,
With charm and laughter, I felt tested.

Like a toddler in a candy store,
I wished for burgers, fries, and more.
But alas, only rainbow sprinkles,
Left me craving those savory wrinkles.

Yet with each jingle, I'd just proclaim,
My heart's desire wasn't all the same.
With quirky flair, I'd dance and sing,
Who knew that joy was a silly thing?

Tangles of Thought

Wrapped around my wrist, a thread,
Of hopes and giggles, lightly spread.
Each knot a memory, bright and bold,
Like socks I lost, secrets untold.

I tugged on dreams like rubber bands,
A stretch, a snap—oh, who understands?
A wish for pizza, covered in cheese,
But I ended with cravings that just wouldn't ease.

In a tangle by the lunchroom door,
I stumbled, laughed, and cried for more.
With salad dreams and burger schemes,
Reality's just not what it seems.

But with each tumble, a giggle flew,
As friends joined in, I found my crew.
We wore mismatched bands, painted in glee,
Cheers to the madness that sets us free!

Artifacts of Ambition

I hung my dreams on a colorful clasp,
A vision lost in a playful grasp.
Each goal a trinket, shiny and bright,
But how to achieve it? Not quite in sight.

With glittering hopes, I marched along,
A parade of thoughts, the humor was strong.
Each step a wish, each wish a chuckle,
But why does life feel like a jigsaw shuffle?

A glitter globe filled with wobbly dreams,
It shapes and shifts, or so it seems.
With a twist of fate and a splash of flair,
I realized ambition needs comic care.

So let us laugh at the plans we map,
For life's a circus and I'm the chap.
With every misstep, a joke I'll share,
In this adventure, we're light as air!

Inspirations in Indigo

In hues of blue where dreams collide,
I found some giggles I couldn't hide.
Each thought a bubble, floating high,
A slapstick wish, oh me, oh my!

Like painting stars with a sippy cup,
I scribbled hopes, oh what a mix-up!
What's this? A wish for a pet giraffe?
But I settled for laughter, it made me laugh.

As indigo fun wrapped round my wrist,
Every chuckle turned into a twist.
With painted fingers, I reached for the sky,
Only to tumble and wave goodbye.

Yet in this laughter, I found my cheer,
Joy wrapped in colors, ever near.
Each goofy wish, a lottery spin,
With every giggle, my heart would grin!

Colors of Aspirations

In colors bright, our dreams take flight,
With silly bands wrapped, oh what a sight!
Each hue a joke, each shade a cheer,
We laugh aloud as goals draw near.

From every twist, a giggle grows,
Red for love, and blue for woes,
A rainbow path of jest we tread,
With silly hopes and laughter spread.

The green for cash, but not a dime,
The yellow gleams like jello slime,
In purple chaos, we find our way,
Chasing blunders, come what may!

So pull the colors, wear them proud,
Make silly wishes, shout out loud!
In every twist, a story spins,
With laughter ringing, let's begin!

Fabric of Futures

In quirky threads, our dreams are sewn,
With laughter stitched, we're never alone,
Each fabric patch, a tale to weave,
We giggle loud, in what we believe.

A pocket of hope with a silly patch,
Laces entwined with a comical catch,
The future's a canvas of colors bright,
With threads of giggles, we craft the light.

From polka dots to stripes so bold,
We wear our dreams, a sight to behold,
Every misstep, a patch on our jeans,
Crafting the fabric of our wild scenes.

So sew these moments, don't let them fade,
In every quirk, a memory made,
With humor's thread, we'll stitch and play,
In life's grand tapestry, we'll find our way!

Adornments of Intent

With trinkets jingle and charms that sway,
We wear our thoughts in a funny way,
A wink and a nudge, a silly grin,
These playful baubles, let laughter begin!

The earrings shout of dreams unspoken,
With rubber bands, our fates are broken,
A necklace of giggles, a bracelet of cheer,
In every adornment, our hopes appear.

From keychains of joy to rings of whack,
We strut about, no looking back,
Each shiny piece holds a punchline true,
Dressed in jest, there's nothing we rue.

So slip on the gems of personality's glee,
Wear the lighthearted like a decree,
With every adornment, a laugh to send,
In the spirit of fun, our messages blend!

Links of Longing

In chains of laughter, we connect our dreams,
With every link, we plot our schemes,
A tug, a twist, with smiles we share,
In every connection, we show we care.

From rubber loops to paperclips tight,
We bind our hopes, holding on with might,
Jokingly linked, in a beautiful mess,
Finding joy in each silly guess.

With laughter's clasp, we form our bonds,
In quirky chains where reality responds,
Each link a memory, a joke we tell,
In the tangle of life, we laugh so well.

So weave those links, let good times flow,
Through funny knots, our spirits grow,
With every chain, a dance we'll find,
In this link of longing, forever entwined!

www.ingramcontent.com/pod-product-compliance
Lightning Source LLC
Chambersburg PA
CBHW060112230426
43661CB00003B/167